SCHIFFER
PUBLISHING

Est. 1974

Inspiring through expert knowledge

Elegant Accents for the Home Garden

Love... ...cap

Hyd...

JOAN HA...

SCHIFFER
PUBLIS...

4880 Lower Valley Road

Library of Congress Control Number: 2024941451

Designed by Beth Oberholtzer
Cover design by Alexa Harris

Type set in Blithe/Ariana Pro/Avenir Next/Baskerville

ISBN: 978-0-7643-6896-7
Printed in China
ePub: 978-1-5073-0538-6

Published by Schiffer Publishing, Ltd.
4880 Lower Valley Road
Atglen, PA 19310
Phone: (610) 593-1777; Fax: (610) 593-2002
Email: info@schifferbooks.com
Web: www.schifferbooks.com

For our complete selection of fine books on this and related subjects, please visit our website at www.schifferbooks.com. You may also write for a free catalog.

Schiffer Publishing's titles are available at special discounts for bulk purchases for sales promotions or premiums. Special editions, including personalized covers, corporate imprints, and excerpts, can be created in large quantities for special needs. For more information, contact the publisher.

To Ashley, Charlotte, and Trixie.
You bring this grandmother great joy.

Disclaimer: Some hydrangea varieties mentioned in this book have trademarked or registered names. They include Abracadabra® Star, BloomStruck®, Cherry Explosion®, Double Delights™ Wedding Gown, Let's Dance Can Do!®, Let's Dance Diva!®, Let's Dance® Starlight, Pop Star™, Seaside Serenade® Cape May, Summer Crush®, Tiny Tuff Stuff™, Tuff Stuff™, Tuff Stuff Ah-Ha®, Tuff Stuff™ Red, Tuff Stuff Top Fun™, Tuxedo® Pink, Twist-n-Shout®, and Wedding Gown®. Their use herein is for identification purposes only. All rights are reserved by their respective owners.

The text and products pictured in this book are from the collection of the author of this book, its publisher, or various private collectors. This book is not sponsored, endorsed, or otherwise affiliated with any of the companies whose products are represented herein. They include Abracadabra® Star, BloomStruck®, Cherry Explosion®, Double Delights™ Wedding Gown, Let's Dance Can Do!®, Let's Dance Diva!®, Let's Dance® Starlight, Pop Star™, Seaside Serenade® Cape May, Summer Crush®, Tiny Tuff Stuff™, Tuff Stuff™, Tuff Stuff Ah-Ha®, Tuff Stuff™ Red, Tuff Stuff Top Fun™, Tuxedo® Pink, Twist-n-Shout®, and Wedding Gown®, among others. This book is derived from the author's independent research.

Contents

Acknowledgment

I am a lucky person indeed, since I have many people in my life who have encouraged and supported my love of hydrangeas over the years. Special thanks go to my sister Maureen Gendrolius, who never toots her own horn but promotes my books with enthusiasm at every opportunity. With humor, wit, and grace she has enhanced my life, most recently as travel companion to the Azores, a longtime bucket list destination for me ever since I learned the islands are covered with hydrangeas. Obrigada, Maureen!

Introduction

Many people automatically think of hydrangeas as big, round, blue or pink flowers calling attention to themselves in garden settings. These are the mopheads, the form commonly associated with the word "hydrangea." The lacecap form, to those previously unfamiliar with it, can seem oddly shaped; somehow not fully formed. Greater familiarity brings appreciation of their gracefully delicate appearance. Despite their exquisite beauty, they are surprisingly sturdy additions to the home garden, and, as a bonus, they are known to attract pollinators. Provide the right conditions and they require little maintenance. Year after year, they produce gorgeous, long-lasting flowers, many of which can be successfully cut for indoor use. They are a gift to yourself and to the environment that keeps on giving. Lovely lacecaps. A world of beauty.

A typical lacecap ('Blau Meister') with sterile sepals surrounding the tiny central fertile flowers

CHAPTER 1

Lacecap FORM

At first glance, the flower head of a lacecap hydrangea seems to be stalled in its growth. Mopheads are the better-known hydrangea form, and people familiar with their appearance, expecting to see fully rounded flower heads, might wonder why this lacecap has not fully developed. But mopheads and lacecaps, while members of the same species—*Hydrangea macrophylla*—are two distinctly different forms within the species.

The flower heads of the lacecap form are composed of an inner section of small, tightly rounded fertile flowers surrounded by larger, more showy, sterile sepals. Those showy sepals in the outer ring do resemble flower petals, but technically they are modified leaves. Their function is to attract pollinators to the fertile flowers in the middle of the inflorescence.

Mopheads have a fuller, more rounded appearance than lacecaps.

This side view of Twist-n-Shout® exhibits the classic lacecap form: a flattened top with an inner ring of small fertile flowers and an outer ring of sterile sepals.

Lacecaps ('White Wave') in the foreground; mopheads ('Enziandom') in the background

Mopheads and lacecaps cozying up to each other in a Nantucket garden

While the two forms, mopheads and lacecaps, look different in appearance, as members of the same species they require the same care, and both are capable of color changes on the basis of the pH of the soil. Since they thrive in the same garden conditions, they make good companions for each other.

The typical lacecap form is of a neat ring of sepals surrounding the central core of the flower head, but there are variations on that theme. Sometimes the sepals are held farther away from the central core on long pedicels, giving it the look of something like a space satellite.

'Shamrock' with its sepals on long pedicels

The white lacecap flowers of Wedding Gown® with 'Nantucket Blue' mopheads

Sometimes the lacecap looks a bit different from the standard form by virtue of double flowers, which describes the appearance when an extra row of sepals surrounds the eye of the floret.

The double flowers of 'Jogasaki'

'Strawberries and Cream' with crowded sepals obscuring the small fertile flowers

'Jogasaki' with the central fertile flowers almost completely obscured by the twisting sepals

'Brestenberg' (mopheads) with Let's Dance Can Do!® (lacecaps). The two forms coexist beautifully together.

H. serrata 'Bluebird'. Sometimes the outer ring of sepals is positioned lower than the central ring of tiny fertile flowers, creating a more rounded look to the inflorescence.

It's not unusual for sterile sepals to pop up in the midst of central fertile flowers.

When considering environmental concerns, it's important to note that the lacecap form is very attractive to pollinators. The relatively flat surface provides an excellent landing surface for insects. This lacecap form appears in several hydrangea species, including *H. arborescens* (also known as smooth hydrangea) and the climbing hydrangea (*H. petiolaris*). In this book we will focus on lacecaps in two species: *H. macrophylla* and *H. serrata*.

'Haas' Halo' is an arborescens variety known to be extremely attractive to pollinators.

'Tokyo Delight'. The bee is attracted to the plant by the showy white sepals, guiding it to the tiny central fertile flowers.

The lacecap-form flowers of climbing hydrangeas (*H. petiolaris*) appear in early spring.

'Fasan'

Wedding Gown®

Let's Dance Diva!®

Twist-n-Shout®

CHAPTER 2

Lacecap
COLOR

Lacecap flowers come in a lovely range of colors, including blue, pink, purple, white, and cherry red. With some varieties, the inner core of small fertile flowers and the outer ring of sepals match in color: pink with pink, white with white, lavender with lavender, blue with blue. (*See facing page*)

Some other varieties sport contrasting colors, such as blue fertile flowers surrounded by white or pink or lavender sepals.

Abracadabra® Star®

'Tokyo Delight'

The flowers of Tuff Stuff™ are known for a richly saturated hue.

'Juno'

'Bits of Lace' in soft pink

'Blue Deckle' is known for the softness of its color.

Flower color ranges from pale, soft colors to deeply saturated colors.

The flower color is affected by the pH of the soil. Blues can become pink in alkaline soil, and pinks can become blue in acidic soil. But even if the color changes, the intensity of the color generally remains the same; deep blues could become deep pink, but not pale pink.

Cherry Explosion® in vibrant cherry pink

Sometimes different colors appear on the same plant, but the intensity of color stays the same, as on 'Blau Meister', shown here.

It can be effective in the garden to combine pale colors with those of a deeper hue.

In an alkaline soil, Let's Dance® Starlight is pink.

Let's Dance® Starlight is blue in an acidic soil.

Twist-n-Shout®. The single pink sepal indicates something going on at the soil level, preventing it from being blue like all the other sepals. Perhaps one tiny section of the roots extended into soil closer to a lawn that had been limed, making it more alkaline.

The plant label suggests 'Zorro' will have blue flowers, but the plant shows a possibly temporary alkaline influence.

White lacecaps are not affected by the pH of the soil. There can be a faint blush of blue or pink on a white lacecap, but that's usually a function of aging rather than soil chemistry. Some color changes can be quite dramatic as the flower ages. For example, Wedding Gown®, which is pure white all summer, eventually ages to deep red.

The color of the flower is what usually draws the eye, but there are a few varieties with striking foliage color, including a recent introduction called Tuxedo® Pink. The leaves are very dark, in such a deep shade of purple that they almost appear black.

'Zorro' in blue

Tuxedo® Pink

'Beauté Vendômoise'

CHAPTER 3
Lacecap Varieties
MACROPHYLLAS

The two dozen macrophylla lacecap varieties presented in this chapter are known for outstanding qualities, making them excellent choices for the home garden. If you are looking for strong performers, ones you can count on to produce healthy beautiful growth year after year, you would do well to select from this set of lacecap hydrangeas.

'Beauté Vendômoise' is an impressively large lacecap bred by Emile Mouillère in 1908. It won the French Certificate of Merit in 1909 and continues to earn rave reviews more than 100 years later. This is a plant with a strong growth habit. The mature size is typically 6 feet high and wide but has been reported growing up to 10 feet high. The flower heads are equally impressive, with prominent sterile sepals arrayed around and over the inner circle of fertile flowers. The sepal color is white tinged with pink or blue as the plant matures, while the inner core of fertile flowers will be pink or blue, depending on the pH of the soil.

'Bits of Lace' was introduced by Novalis Nursery in 2005 and is described as *Hydrangea × serratophylla*, which means it is a hybrid resulting from a cross between *Hydrangea macrophylla* and *Hydrangea serrata*. The inclusion of serrata blood indicates it will be more cold hardy than pure macrophyllas. The lovely lacecap flowers are set off by deep-green foliage. The shrub itself will grow to be 3–5 feet high and wide.

'Bits of Lace'

'Blaumeise', an award-winning lacecap from the Teller series, is sometimes referred to as 'Teller Blue'. This variety is known for large (up to 8 inches) deep-blue flowers with long-lasting color. The shrub is upright and vigorous with dark shiny leaves, maturing to 5 feet tall and wide. It received the AGM (Award of Garden Merit) from the Royal Horticultural Society.

'Blaumeise'

The abundant flowers of 'Blaumeise'

'Blue Cassell', introduced in 2010, is a compact lacecap maturing to the 4–5-foot range. Beautiful in blue with large flowers supported by sturdy stems, it is similar to the Teller lacecaps. The flowers face up toward the sun above deep-green foliage.

'Blue Wave' is a classic lacecap bred by Victor Lemoine in 1904. It can be quite a tall shrub, over 6 feet tall and wide at maturity, and is a good choice when creating a hedge. With glossy dark-green foliage, it is known to do well in coastal gardens and has flowers that dry well, sometimes to a silvery blue. The variety is a seedling of 'Mariesii' and is also known as 'Mariesii Perfecta'. It received the AGM (Award of Garden Merit) from the Royal Horticultural Society in 1992.

'Blue Wave'

'Blue Cassell'

'Blue Wave' might seem like a misnomer when the flower is lavender purple.

'Fasan'

Cherry Explosion®

Cherry Explosion® was introduced by Star® Roses and Plants in 2017, offering cherry-red lacecap flowers on a compact plant. At maturity it is about 3 feet high and wide, making it appropriate in containers as well as a front-of-the-border plant in the garden. Note that in acidic soil the flowers can be more purple than red. The flowers are impressively large for such a compact plant and are beautifully paired with dark-green foliage.

'Fasan' is a classic red or deep-pink lacecap (purple in acidic soil) with large flowers held aloft on sturdy stems. It is part of the Teller series and is sometimes referred to as 'Teller Red'. Double rows of sterile flowers encircle the small, fertile flowers and do well as cut flowers. It has an upright habit, maturing to about 5 feet tall and wide.

Side view of 'Fasan'

'Izu no Hana' gets its name from the place where it was discovered: the Izu Peninsula, south of Tokyo. It was discovered in the wild around 1970, and its Japanese name means "flower of Izu." 'Izu no Hana' has several attractive features, especially its double flowers on long pedicels, which extend away from the central core of tiny fertile flowers. The foliage is glossy dark green, which can, under the right conditions, take on autumn coloration. Both the flowers and the shrub itself are on the small side. Expect the plant to stay compact at about 4 feet tall and wide.

'Izu no Hana'

'Jogasaki'

'Jogasaki', like 'Izu no Hana', has double flowers on long pedicels. They are dissimilar, though, both in overall shrub size ('Jogasaki' is larger, maturing at 5 × 5 feet) and flower size (larger flowers than 'Izu no Hana', with blooms up to 8 inches). This is a strong, wind-hardy plant discovered on the Izu Peninsula near Cape Jogasaki. Its leaves have a reddish cast with a central red vein.

'Kardinal'

The name of this variety, 'Lady in Red', can seem misleading when the flowers are blue, as they are likely to be when the soil is acidic, but the name relates primarily to the reddish stems and veins.

'Kardinal' is a red-flowering lacecap (purple in acidic soil) with deep-green foliage. It is a sturdy, upright shrub with strong stems, like other hydrangeas in the Teller series. This one was introduced in 1989. The flowers are large, with vibrant color, and work well as cut flowers. A vigorous grower, it achieved the AGM (Award of Garden Merit) from the Royal Horticultural Society.

'Lady in Red', known for red stems and red central veins in the leaves, was a 2004 University of Georgia introduction. Both the flowers and the foliage turn to burgundy red in the fall. This is a reliably cold-hardy variety, a hybrid with serrata blood. It grows up to 6 feet tall and wide, with deep-green leaves. Recognized as a good breeding partner, it was used in the breeding of Twist-n-Shout®, BloomStruck®, and Summer Crush®.

'Lady in Red' in fall coloration

'Lanarth White'

Let's Dance Diva!®

'Lanarth White', discovered in Lanarth, Cornwall, tolerates sunny conditions in a coastal setting. It is a medium-size shrub producing a profusion of creamy white lacecap flowers with pale-green foliage. This variety achieved the Royal Horticultural Society's Award of Garden Merit in 1993.

Let's Dance Diva!® has flowers that are surprisingly large on such a small plant. At maturity, this variety is only 2–3 feet tall and wide, but because of the flower size it has a big impact. This would be a great choice for a container. The flowers will be soft pink or blue, depending on the pH of the soil, and do well as cut flowers. This is a mounding plant with sturdy stems and dark-green foliage. It was introduced by Proven Winners® in 2013.

Let's Dance® Starlight is a very pretty lacecap, flowering in pink or blue, depending on the pH of the soil, and makes a good cut flower. The shrub tends to stay small, in the 2-to-3-foot range (height and width), but can grow larger given the right conditions. The flowers are large, the foliage is deep green, and the plant has a mounding habit. It was introduced by Proven Winners.

Let's Dance® Starlight

'Libelle' has been acclaimed as an outstanding white lacecap. Part of the Teller series, it is sometimes called 'Teller White'. Its large blooms are made up of full white sepals surrounding blue fertile flowers, creating a stunning contrast. It achieves a mature size of 5 feet tall and wide, with glossy green leaves. The Royal Horticultural Society honored it with its AGM (Award of Garden Merit).

'Lilacina', also known as 'Mariesii Lilacina', was introduced by Victor Lemoine in 1904. This variety is a strong, vigorous grower with an upright habit, maturing to 5 feet (height and width), but can grow larger with the right conditions. The flowers, often in shades of plum or lavender, are good for drying since they hold their colors well. The foliage is light green, and the stems are purple speckled.

'Libelle

'Lilacina'. *Photo courtesy of Joan Brazeau*

'Shamrock'

'Shamrock' was introduced by Corinne Mallet of the Shamrock Collection in France. It is a double-flowered lacecap with an irregular array of flowers on long pedicels erupting beautifully from the central core of fertile flowers. This is a compact variety growing 3–4 feet tall and wide. The flowers are pink or violet, depending on the soil. It has an upright habit and would work well as a specimen plant.

'Star Gazer' is part of the Double Delights™ series and is also known as Double Delights™ Star Gazer. Hybridized by T. Yamamoto in Japan, it is an eye-catching variety with a profusion of double flowers in pink or blue (depending on the soil) held on long pedicels above the fertile flowers. White picotee edges add to the beauty of the flowers. This is a compact variety (3–4 feet) with a mounding habit.

'Star Gazer'

'Tokyo Delight' was first encountered by the author in England in the Lake District at Holehird Gardens, the site of a national hydrangea collection. Even with hydrangea beauty abounding all around, this variety stood out. The shrub was upright, standing about 6 feet tall, and was loaded with small, delicate white lacecap flowers that fluttered like butterflies in the light breeze. It was clear why the word "delight" figured in its name. The variety has been around for a long time, said to have been introduced before 1940. With its fall color, it is suspected to be a hybrid with *Hydrangea serrata*. It received the Award of Garden Merit from the Royal Horticultural Society.

Twist-n-Shout® is a reblooming lacecap introduced as part of the Endless Summer® collection. A cross between the hydrangeas 'Penny Mac' and 'Lady in Red', it blooms on both old and new wood in deep pink or periwinkle blue, depending on the pH of the soil. Additional color is provided by sturdy deep-red stems and deep-green foliage that turns maroon red in the fall. The upright and rounded shrub matures to 3–5 feet high and 3–4 feet wide.

Twist-n-Shout®

'Tokyo Delight'

'Veitchii'

'Veitchii' was imported from Japan by Charles Maries for his employer, the Veitch Nursery, and was introduced in 1880. The big, white, sterile flowers surround contrasting blue fertile flowers, creating a stunning effect. The award-winning compact plant is used extensively in breeding due to cold-hardiness and mildew resistance. It is an excellent cut flower and dried flower and received the AGM (Award of Garden Merit) from the RHS.

Wedding Gown®

'White Wave'

Wedding Gown® is part of the Double Delights™ series, and as such it is known as Double Delights™ Wedding Gown. This is a compact variety, maturing to 3–4 feet high. A profusion of white double flowers cover the plant, creating the effect of a dense collection of bridal bouquets. The flowers turn deep red in the fall and dry well in that color. The variety received the AGM (Award of Garden Merit) from the RHS.

'White Wave', the floriferous lacecap originally known as 'Mariesii Grandiflora', was bred by Victor Lemoine in France in 1902. It picked up the name 'White Wave' along the way, a good description of the effect of the large white flowers massed above dark-green foliage. 'White Wave' is a sister plant to other seedlings of 'Mariesii', including 'Blue Wave' and 'Lilacina'. The plant matures to a substantial 5 feet high and wide, with flowers produced over an extended period. It should be protected from intense afternoon sun. In 1992 it received the AGM (Award of Garden Merit) from the RHS.

'Zorro' is another hydrangea that has won the coveted Award of Garden Merit (AGM) from the Royal Horticultural Society. Introduced in 2009, it matures to 4–5 feet tall and wide, with distinctive purple-black stems sturdily supporting large, showy flowers in deep blue or bright pink, depending on the soil. This variety would make an eye-catching specimen in a decorative container, or as a focal point in a landscape setting. The foliage is a glossy dark green, changing to fall colors as the summer season ends.

'Zorro'

'Zorro' with its purple-black stems

'Blue Billow'

CHAPTER 4

Lacecap Varieties
SERRATAS

The previous chapter featured a selection of lacecaps in the *Hydrangea macrophylla* species. This chapter focuses on a different species, *Hydrangea serrata*, also known as mountain hydrangeas. While the macrophyllas and serratas are similar in appearance, there are some key differences to be noted.

A large percentage of hydrangeas originated in Japan. Macrophyllas (also known as big-leaf hydrangeas) originated in coastal areas at low elevations, while the serratas originated in mountainous regions. Not surprisingly, the serratas, accustomed to high elevations, are more cold hardy than macrophyllas. This is a significant feature, especially for hydrangea lovers who live in some of the colder hardiness zones. The buds of the serratas are more likely to survive the cold of winter and produce flowers in the spring. Not only that, but serratas tend to stay dormant longer than the macrophyllas and are thus more likely to survive late-spring frosts.

The serrata lacecap flowers look very much like those of the macrophylla species, but the shrubs themselves are usually smaller than macrophyllas. A bonus feature is autumn color in the foliage. If the leaves of a macrophylla exhibit colorful changes in the fall, it is a clue that the variety might have some serrata blood.

'Blue Billow' resulted from wild seed collected by Richard Lighty in Korea with seedlings raised at the Mt. Cuba Research Station in Delaware. This lacecap variety is on the small side, known for clean foliage and deep reddish-purple fall color. It matures to about 4 feet tall, with a wide spread, and is covered with abundant flowers. It blooms reliably, with large light-blue flower heads held atop sturdy stems. The plant has an attractive mounding habit and does well in a filtered shade setting.

'Bluebird' is taller than the typical serrata, known to mature to 6 feet tall in areas hospitable to hydrangeas, such as Cape Cod. This is an award-winning hydrangea, receiving the AGM (Award of Garden Merit) from the RHS in 1992. The blue or pink flowers, despite being fairly small, create a showy effect by covering the shrub. The dark-green leaves mature to copper-bronze tones in autumn. The sepals, arranged in fours, resemble four-leaf clovers.

'Blue Deckle' derives its name from its deckle-edged sepals in soft powder blue. It is a dwarf variety bred by noted hydrangea expert Michael Haworth-Booth. It is known for good flowering, often producing a light second bloom in the fall. The changing season also produces a change in foliage color from green to reddish purple. Expect this shrub to grow no more than 3–4 feet tall.

'Bluebird'

'Blue Deckle'

'Diadem'

'Grayswood'

'Diadem' is an early-to-flower compact shrub (height about 3 feet) with small, delicate flowers. It blooms well, including many lateral flowers. The serrated leaves provide lovely fall foliage. This variety holds up well in hot, sunny conditions. A good choice for a decorative container but also good at the front of a garden border.

'Grayswood' was introduced in England from Japan in 1881. A retired China merchant, Benjamin Ellis Coates Chambers, bought Grayswood Hill House in 1880 and soon began planting the garden with trees and shrubs, including this lovely serrata. This variety is tall and slender, maturing to 5–6 feet, with white flowers gradually changing to deep pink. In the fall the flowers turn over to reveal deep-crimson color, and the foliage provides autumn color as well. This sturdy, frost-hardy variety received the AGM (Award of Garden Merit) in 1993.

Let's Dance Can Do!® in pink

Let's Dance Can Do!® in blue

Let's Dance Can Do!® produces flower buds all along the stem, not just at the top of the stem, reducing worries about lack of flowers after a tough winter kills off part of the plant. The semidouble starlike flowers themselves are large and brightly colored; either rich violet purple or bubblegum pink, depending on the soil. The plant is medium in size, typically growing to 4 feet, with a spread of 3 feet, and is known for being cold hardy. With a mounding habit, the shrub is filled with flowers that are good both as cut flowers and as dried flowers. It was introduced by Proven Winners in 2021 and was formerly known as Let's Dance Can Can.

'Purple Tiers' is a showstopper despite its small size. Vivid double flowers resemble colorful stars atop long pedicels. In acidic soil the flower color is usually a rich purple, but if a lot of aluminum is present in the soil, the flowers might be more blue than purple. Expect pink flowers in an alkaline soil. They are good cut flowers, and they also dry well. The shrub is compact,

'Purple Tiers'

maturing to 3–4 feet. The flowers bloom from midsummer to frost, with both the flower heads and the foliage turning red in the fall. A good front-of-the-border plant, and also a good choice for containers. It was introduced around 1950 by Isamu Satoh and is also known as 'Miyama Yae Murasaki'.

Seaside Serenade® Cape May features large, showy lacecap blooms supported on thick, sturdy stems. The flowers are good as cut flowers. This is a compact mounding variety, maturing to 3 feet tall and wide (and possibly 4 feet under the right conditions). The deep-green serrated foliage turns burgundy in the fall. It is a 2017 Monrovia introduction.

Seaside Serenade® Cape May in blue

Seaside Serenade® Cape May in pink

Tiny Tuff Stuff™

Tuff Stuff™

Tiny Tuff Stuff™ is a surprisingly sturdy plant despite the delicate appearance of its double flowers. Because of its bud-hardiness, it produces an abundance of flowers in soft shades of blue or pink, depending on the soil. It is a small plant with a mounding habit, maturing to about 2 feet tall and wide. This is a good choice for a container or front-of-the-border placement, planting 18 inches apart.

An abundance of flowers on Tiny Tuff Stuff™

Tuff Stuff™ is a fairly small plant with a large presence due to abundant blooming. The mature size of the shrub is 2–3 feet, with a tidy mounded habit. The flowers are bright pink or deep purplish blue, depending on the pH of the soil. The foliage is dark green.

Tuff Stuff™ is the original plant in the Tuff Stuff collection, which includes Tiny Tuff Stuff™ and Tuff Stuff Ah-Ha®. The most recent addition to the series is called Tuff Stuff Top Fun™.

Tuff Stuff Ah-Ha® has impressively large flowers despite the overall small size of the plant. This is a mounding plant that grows 2–3 feet high and 2–3 feet wide. The sepals surrounding the central fertile flowers have been compared to water lilies in appearance. The flowers can be pink or blue, depending on the pH of the soil, and the plants can be used as edging plants in the home garden.

Abundant blooms on Tuff Stuff™ in a home garden on Cape Cod

Tuff Stuff Ah-Ha®

Lacecap hydrangeas complement the mophead hydrangeas painted on the mailbox.

CHAPTER 5

Lacecaps
IN THE LANDSCAPE

Lacecap hydrangeas satisfy a wide range of landscaping needs and desires. Consider their virtues. They can look delicate or bold, with colors ranging from softly pale to vibrantly assertive. Their size range allows for placement anywhere in the home garden, including petite front-of-the-border varieties, a substantial collection of midsized shrubs, and impressively tall varieties available for background plants. They are low maintenance and adaptable for planting in containers. They can be attention-getting specimen plants, or one of many as part of an effective mass-planting display.

The photos in this chapter were selected to show some of the countless ways that lacecaps can be used effectively to enhance the home garden.

Some points to consider when deciding on placement include hardscape accents, companion planting, and viewing angles.

Hardscape Accents

Permanent features in your landscape, such as fences, stone walls, and decorative structures, can be excellent foils for lacecap hydrangeas.

White backgrounds are particularly good for making flower colors pop.

Lacecaps flowing over a fence separating the front yard from the backyard

The lacecaps look good on both sides of the fence.

Twist-n-Shout® surrounding the succulents planted in a birdbath

Lacecaps massed in front of a Cape Cod church, creating a solid, unifying effect

Several lacecap varieties in a residential border

Companion Planting

Lacecaps can be placed effectively next to or in the midst of other plants, including different varieties of hydrangeas.

Tuff Stuff™ Red, featured in this backyard border

In a container, a lacecap plays the role of thriller along with plant companions acting as fillers and spillers.

A river of lacecaps flowing amid a variety of evergreens

Lacecaps mixed
with mopheads
in a Nantucket
border

Tiny Tuff Stuff™ with contrasting companion flowers

Massed flowers make a strong statement, especially with contrasting colors.

Viewing Angles

Lacecaps are often visually stunning when viewed from the side or from above. Placing them near a window allows viewing from inside the house as well as from outside: a bonus. When possible, place them in high-traffic areas, where their beautiful flowers can be appreciated at close range.

The side view of Abracadabra® Star® is visually striking, with its black stems demanding attention.

'Blaumeise' as seen from above when standing on the porch

This 'Blaumeise' was placed strategically to allow the flowers to be seen from the side when walking to the porch steps, and from above when standing on the porch.

Pink lacecaps viewed from above

Tuff Stuff Ah-Ha® viewed from above

Blue lacecaps lining a fence in a side yard on Martha's Vineyard. Anyone passing by on the sidewalk is treated to a good close-up view of the beautiful flowers.

'Lilacina' viewed through a dining-room window. *Photo courtesy of Joan Brazeau*

Take some time when deciding on placement of hydrangeas in your garden. In addition to the factors mentioned above, remember to plan for the mature size of the variety you've selected. You want it to work not just on planting day but every day thereafter.

Lush raspberry-purple lacecaps cascading over a fence in Orleans, Massachusetts

A close-up view of lacecap flowers along a Martha's Vineyard sidewalk

The flowers of 'Game Changer' are distinctly larger than those of Tuff Stuff™ (blue) and 'Wedding Gown' (white).

CHAPTER 6
Lacecap
SIZE

If you are thinking of adding one or more lacecaps to your garden, it's a good idea to take size into consideration, both flower size and overall plant size. Both these variables influence the impact that a particular variety may have in the home landscape.

Flower Size

Lacecap flowers range from small and dainty to impressively large. Both the size of the flowers and the effect you are trying to create can help you decide on placement in the landscape. Sometimes there is a direct correlation between the size of the plant and the size of its flowers, but not always. It's somewhat surprising how many low-to-the-ground compact shrubs produce dramatically oversized flowers. Conversely, large shrubs can be covered in small blooms. Flower size tends to be consistent for individual varieties, but there can be occasional over- or underachievers.

Big impact can frequently be achieved with large flowers. Lacecap varieties known to produce large flowers include 'Beauté Vendômoise', 'Blaumeise', 'Blue Wave', Cherry Explosion®, 'Fasan', 'Fuji Waterfall', 'Game Changer', 'Taube', Tuff Stuff Ah-Ha®, and 'White Wave'.

'Beauté Vendômoise'

A sepal from 'Beauté Vendômoise'

A leaf from 'Beauté Vendômoise'

Tuff Stuff Ah-Ha®

Cherry Explosion®

Lacecap flowers tend to be whichever size is characteristic of the variety. A variety known for medium-size flowers, such as this one ('Blue Cassell'), will primarily produce that size, but exceptions are possible, with the occasional very large or very small flower.

Despite its low profile, Cherry Explosion® is noticeable because of its large flowers.

Tuff Stuff Ah-Ha® with one exceptionally large flower

'Wedding Gown'. One flower alone can create the effect of a wedding bouquet.

The flowers of 'Blaumeise' can be quite large.

'Wedding Gown' stays low to the ground but has a big impact because of the abundance of flowers.

Overall Plant Size

Before installing a plant in your landscape, you should take into account its projected size at maturity. It's frustrating to have to move a plant that has grown too big for its location. You want to avoid negative developments, such as a view being blocked or a path overgrown. Better to put the right plant in the right place from the start.

Fortunately, breeders of plants learn from observation and experience how big particular varieties are likely to get, and this information is routinely shared with consumers. You just have to pay attention to that information before planting day in your garden.

Lacecap hydrangeas range in height from 2 feet to well over 6 feet. This information is an important factor in deciding which one to put at the front of a border, which to plant in a container, which to use as a specimen plant, and so on. Gardeners need to have good imaginations. You need to be able to picture a plant in full mature glory in your mind's eye before it ever goes into the ground. This is particularly important when the plant you've found at the garden center is a little thing in a 1-gallon pot. It will grow!

Tuff Stuff™ has a low profile with abundant blooming.

Most lacecaps mature in the 4–5-foot range. Many but not all of these are the same in width as they are in height. A simple notation like this on a plant label: 5×5′, indicates a plant that will eventually grow to be 5 feet tall and 5 feet wide. Most gardeners are experienced enough to anticipate the height. It's the width that can take them by surprise. Both dimensions are important for planning purposes.

Representative lists of lacecaps by mature size are included here to aid in decision-making. Keep in mind that each variety has a typical mature size, but they could be smaller in poor conditions or larger in ideal conditions.

Tuff Stuff™

A shorter lacecap variety would have been a better choice to be planted under this window.

Small Lacecap Shrubs (under 4 feet)

'Blue Billow'
'Blue Deckle'
Cherry Explosion®
'Diadem'
'Fuji Waterfall'
'Izu no Hana'
Let's Dance Diva!®
Let's Dance® Starlight
'Purple Tiers'
Seaside Serenade® Cape May
'Shamrock'
'Stargazer'
Tiny Tuff Stuff™
Tuff Stuff™
Tuff Stuff Ah-Ha®
Tuff Stuff™ Red'
'Wedding Gown'

Medium Lacecap Shrubs (4-5 feet)

'Bits of Lace'
'Blaumeise'
'Blue Cassell'
'Fasan'
'Jogasaki'
'Kardinal'
'Lanarth White'
Let's Dance Can Do!®
'Libelle'
Twist-n-Shout®
'Veitchii'
'White Wave'
'Zorro'

The owners of this corner residential property left enough space between these lacecaps to allow them to spread out to about 5 feet wide.

Large Lacecap Shrubs (5 feet and taller)

'Beauté Vendômoise'
'Bluebird'
'Blue Wave'
'Geoffrey Chadbund'
'Grayswood'
'Lady in Red'
'Lilacina'
'Tokyo Delight'

This lacecap planted in the front yard of a Cape Cod home has plenty of room to grow to whatever size it wants to be.

Here is a lacecap on Martha's Vineyard that was placed well to allow its mature size.

During the Cape Cod Hydrangea Festival, this Let's Dance® Starlight is a showstopper, the subject of many photos. The variety usually stays small, but here it is an overachiever. The homeowners report it has been grown in the same pot for about ten years.

The author was one of many visitors happy to pose with Let's Dance® Starlight.

Let's Dance® Starlight, impressive in size in its container, is easily spotted from a distance.

As noted, flower size and overall shrub size influence the impact the plant has in the garden. There is another factor to consider: floral abundance. Some varieties are known for being consistently smothered in flowers. The following lacecap varieties are known for the kind of abundant blooms that will be sure to attract the eye of the garden visitor.

Lacecaps with Abundant Blooms

'Blue Wave'
'Fasan'
'Lanarth White'
Tuff Stuff™
'Wedding Gown'
'White Wave'

When conditions are ideal, hydrangeas can grow to impressive sizes. These two plants are located right across the street from the Hyannis ferry terminal on Cape Cod.

Floral changes in autumn

CHAPTER 7

Lacecap
LIFE CYCLE

Spring has sprung with hydrangeas when you see fresh green growth appearing along the stem. It is a reassuring sign that the shrub has survived the winter and is beginning the process of development that will eventually produce beautiful flowers for seasonal enjoyment.

In early spring the first hint of a lacecap flower emerges, tucked into a large leaf bouquet and looking more vegetable than floral; broccoli comes to mind. With green blending into green, it gives little indication of the beauty soon to come.

Fresh green growth in spring

The first growth is all green.

What was all green gradually takes on color. Shape-changing occurs as well. The flower that evolves from that tight little clump of broccoli is stunning in its beauty, with large flowers (sepals, really) encircling tiny fertile flowers.

The lacecap flower generously lingers a long time in its most glorious form before swan diving into its final faded autumn appearance, with outer sepals drooping upside down in muted colors. The cycle for the season is complete.

A summer lacecap flower

The colors that appear first in the spring are usually soft pastels. It takes awhile—possibly several weeks—before the flower develops full, rich tones of blue or purple or pink.

In early spring, Twist-n-Shout® presents itself in soft, pale tones (*top photo*), which gradually change to the deeper rich colors of summer (*bottom photo*).

The tiny star-shaped balls of fertile flowers at the central core of the flower hold pollen and can produce seeds. They will gradually loosen, frequently exploding into a more distinct star shape. Each variety explodes in its own distinctive way. (The author thinks of this process in terms of explosions, but variations of this word are not used universally. Others might describe it less dramatically by mentioning the fertile flowers "opening up.")

'Strawberries and Cream' in an early stage of development, with tightly enclosed fertile flowers surrounded by the larger and more-colorful sepals

'Blaumeise', with fertile flowers in the center starting to explode

It's not just the tiny fertile flowers that are exploding. The eyes at the center of the surrounding sepals open as well. Depending on the lacecap variety, these might develop into fertile florets.

The next stage is marked by the upside-down movement of the large outer ring of sepals. The sepals are no longer held rigidly aloft but are bending, bending, until they hang limply upside down. The flower has clearly reached its antique stage.

Side view of exploding fertile flowers

The blue eyes in the center of the white sepals are starting to explode.

'Blue Wave' shown at two different stages: early August (*top photo*) and late August (*bottom photo*), on Cape Cod

Tokyo Delight' shown in midsummer (*top photo*) and late summer (*bottom photo*)

There can be differences in appearance from the early antique phase to a later phase. Colors may deepen, or sepals may become spotted.

'White Wave' in early August, Cape Cod

❮ 'Wedding Gown' goes through several color changes as the seasons progress, from pure white to deep red, with a variety of color changes along the way.

'White Wave' first turns its sepals upside down as it ages (*top photo*), and later, these sepals may become spotted (*bottom photo*). These two photos were taken in late August (1) and late September (2) on Cape Cod.

A graceful blue lacecap with sepals starting to turn upside down in autumn

Each flower goes through the life cycle sequence individually. It's not unusual to have flowers at different stages of development adjacent to each other on the same plant.

The two flowers, side by side on the shrub, are at different stages of development.

The same plant can look very different, depending on when you see it during the growing season. This lacecap has blue flowers through spring and summer, but the flowers fade to pink in the fall, and the sepals turn upside down.

It can be fascinating to observe the lacecap flower at all stages in its life cycle, but most gardeners are content to know that the flower will provide satisfying beauty in the home landscape throughout the growing season.

Lacecap plants offered for
sale outside a supermarket

CHAPTER 8

Lacecaps

INDOORS

At most times of the year, you can enjoy the beauty of lacecap hydrangeas indoors, provided your local florist stocks them along with the more commonly provided cut flowers and greenery. Forced hydrangeas (sometimes called florist hydrangeas) are widely available at Easter and Mother's Day, and now, due to increased popularity, they are offered at other times of the year as well. Many florists will try to accommodate special requests, including the form of hydrangea you prefer (mophead or lacecap) and the flower color (blue, pink, purple, or white). White hydrangeas are often available at Christmas time since they pair so well with red flowers.

There are advantages to decorating indoor spaces with these potted hydrangeas. The flowers provide beautiful color for weeks, and even when the color has faded to muted shades, the flower form holds up, supported by long-lasting foliage. Depending on the variety, the lacecap you bring home from the florist could provide you with beautiful color for several weeks up to two months.

'First White'

Some people throw out the plant when the flowers are spent, but there is no need to do that if you have a garden. They can be planted outside (in zones 5–9), where they may come back year after year. There's no guarantee of that, because they tend to be less hardy than the hydrangeas specifically produced for garden use, but it can't hurt to try, and some of them succeed surprisingly well.

An alternative to planting in the garden is to place the plant during its dormant season in an unheated garage or shed or basement, where it will be protected from harsh winter conditions. The author has many hydrangeas, mopheads and lacecaps, that spend the winter in the garage and are moved to containers in a courtyard during the growing season. It's very satisfying to see old favorites return to bloom year after year.

'Strawberries and Cream'

Abracadabra® Star®

This plant was placed on a low pedestal to allow viewing from above.

Cut blooms work well in a variety of containers.

Cut Flowers

Another way to enjoy lacecaps indoors is as cut flowers, either purchased from a florist or harvested from your own garden shrubs. Lacecaps can look wonderful in interesting containers.

The solid-white container is perfect for all flower colors.

Sometimes the container dictates what color of flower would look best inside.

You can choose to display lacecaps alone, or mixed with mopheads of the same or a contrasting color.

Indoor displays can easily be changed seasonally. These are dried 'Wedding Gown' flowers in an autumn hue.

Some lacecap flowers are so large, only one flower is needed to fill a vase. Smaller flowers can be used effectively with other flowers and frequently appear in floral bouquets for sale at farmers' markets and in grocery stores.

If you plan to cut some flowers in your own garden, try to remember to give the plant a good soaking the night before, and cut the flowers early in the morning. There's no need to make the arrangement right away, but do place the flowers (stripped of their leaves) in water until it's time to arrange them.

This one will be cut to join others in an indoor arrangement.

Let's Dance Can Do!®
(previously named Let's Dance Can Can)

Sometimes a single flower is large enough to fill a small container.

Tuff Stuff™

Lacecaps shortly after a summer downpour. This is a great time to cut the flowers for indoor use, when they are filled with water just after a good soaking.

'Bluebird'

Pop Star™

Near the end of the growing season, consider drying some lacecap flowers for indoor use during the colder months. They can provide some much-needed color after the garden has been put to bed for the winter.

'Wedding Gown'

The following lacecap varieties are known to do especially well as cut flowers.
   'Fasan'
   'Geoffrey Chadbund'
   'Kardinal'
   Let's Dance Can Do!®
   Let's Dance Diva!®
   Let's Dance® Starlight
   'Purple Tiers'
   'Rotdrossel'
   Seaside Serenade® Cape May
   Tuff Stuff Ah-Ha®
   'Veitchii'
   'Wedding Gown' (a.k.a. Double Delights™ Wedding Gown)

Lacecaps and mopheads can be brought indoors for drying at the same time, in late summer.

Lacecaps take very little time to dry.

Some lacecaps that dry well are
    'Blaumeise'
    'Blue Wave'
    'Eisvogel'
    Let's Dance Can Do!®
    'Lilacina'

    Tuff Stuff Ah-Ha®
    'Veitchii'
    'Wedding Gown'
    'Zaunkoenig'

Some lacecap varieties can appear quite different as the seasons change. This blue-and-white combination is made up of the mophead 'Hamburg' and the lacecap 'Wedding Gown', cut for indoor use during the summer. The dried flowers in the white milk-glass container are also 'Hamburg' and 'Wedding Gown', in the deep-red color they develop in the fall.

'Beauté Vendômoise'

CHAPTER 9
Lacecap
SUCCESS

Home gardeners know to expect some failures along with their successes. With all the variables and experimentation involved, they know that some plants will not perform as planned. The information in this chapter is designed to increase the likelihood of your having success with your lacecap hydrangeas.

Good variety selection is the first step toward success with lacecaps. A good variety is one that suits your garden conditions and the particular location you have in mind. It is the right size to fit into the space now and has sufficient space to keep growing until it reaches its full mature size. It will flower well in the amount of sunlight available to it during the day. It will be compatible with nearby plantings. It has a tried-and-true reputation as a reliable garden performer. And, most important, its appearance makes you happy.

'Wedding Gown'

Abracadabra® Star®

Learn as much as you can before the purchasing and planting stages. Plant labels are very helpful at point of purchase. A great deal of very helpful information can be packed into a small space. At the very least, the label should tell you sunlight requirements and size at maturity, but many labels provide other useful bits of information. For example, the label for 'Bits of Lace' mentions the expected flower color (pink), the plant's habit (compact), information about the foliage (shiny), flower size (large), tolerance for full sun (good), soil requirements (poor soil is okay), where it thrives (by the sea), what size to expect the plant to be at maturity (4–5 feet tall and 4 feet wide), and pointers toward pruning (blooms on old and new growth). That is a lot of helpful information.

Keep in mind, though, that plant labels can mislead by what they omit to say. In the 'Bits of Lace' example, the label indicates the expected flower color is pink. What they don't say is that the flower color is actually dependent on the pH of the soil and the presence or absence of aluminum. Labels that do include the pH factor express it in different ways: "vivid pink (or blue depending upon pH)"; "Will bloom pink or blue depending on soil chemistry"; "This lacecap is dark pink in alkaline soils and dark lavender in acidic soils"; or "Lacy deep-pink centers are surrounded by gorgeous blossoms of pink or periwinkle blue, depending on soil type."

AGWAY 20

Hydrangea macrophylla BITS OF LACE

Bits of Lace Hydrangea

Pink lace-cap flowers
Compact with large flower heads
Blooms on old & new growth
Boasts all the great attributes of 'Lanarth White' with shinier foliage and larger flowers
Good in full sun, poor soil and by the sea
Mature 4-5' x 4'

Tuff Stuff™

"Hardy to zone 5" in a plant's description can also mislead by what it doesn't say. It can be plant hardy without promising bud-hardiness. In other words, the cold of winter might not kill off the plant, but it might kill off the flower buds, meaning the plant might appear healthy, achieving its usual shape with lots of green foliage, but you won't get any flowers. The plant survived; the flowers did not. The hydrangea macrophylla label that says "Hardy to zone 5" to be truly helpful should add something like "*Bud hardy* to zone 7." Lacecaps are more likely to succeed in zones 7–9. If you don't know your zone, check with a local garden center. Some winter plant protection might be needed in colder zones.

AGWAY

Hydrangea macrophylla 'Kompeito'

DOUBLE DELIGHTS STAR GAZER HYDRANGEA

Unique lacecap with blue or pink star insets, depending on soil pH, surrounded by white picotee edges
Compact growth habit
Features fully double blooms supported by extra strong stems
Mature: Fast grower to 3-4' tall and 3-5' wide
Exposure: Filtered to partial sun

This label for Double Delights™ Star Gazer does indicate the influence of soil pH on flower color.

The color of the actual flower (in this case, 'Zorro') doesn't always match the color on the label. A helpful label explains that flower color is dependent on the pH of the soil. Check on the reverse of the label for full information.

Lacecaps in ideal conditions: morning sun and afternoon shade

Tuff Stuff™ color lasts longer when shaded from afternoon sun.

White lacecap flowers are prone to scorching and turning brown if subjected to intense afternoon sun. 'Wedding Gown' stays pure white when protected from the sun.

A vibrant pink lacecap would fade quickly with too much sun, especially afternoon sun.

Sunlight

Most lacecaps thrive in morning sun and afternoon shade. You might not have those ideal conditions in your own yard. Let's say your only garden space gets full sun all day. Most lacecaps will not be happy in that situation, especially in the full heat of the summer months. You will need to look for a variety identified as being tolerant of full sun (see 'Bits of Lace' above), but even then, chances of success are iffy. Most lacecaps are low-maintenance plants, but any plant under stress may become high maintenance. You will need to provide plenty of moisture and possibly even portable shade (think umbrellas and the like) to help those stressed plants get through the challenging conditions successfully.

Conversely, lacecaps in full shade will be easy to maintain, with lush, healthy foliage, but don't expect any flowers. Hydrangeas need several hours of sunlight to produce a good floral display.

Conditions can change over time in a garden. The author once bought a property where trees provided cover for hydrangeas in a front yard flower bed. The trees helped create the ideal conditions of morning sun and afternoon shade, and the hydrangeas thrived. A few years later the trees became diseased and had to be cut down. The hydrangeas were now subjected to full sun, and, not surprisingly, they became stressed. Fortunately, the plants seemed to adapt to their less-than-ideal space. With extra attention paid to the moisture needs of the plants (involving watering and mulching), attractive flower production continued. The intense afternoon sun did produce some negative consequences. Flower color faded sooner than it did in ideal conditions, and there was some scorching of flowers after particularly hot days. The blooms were no longer candidates to be brought indoors for dried arrangements, because their color was too washed out.

It's also important to note that a newly planted hydrangea will not be as resilient as one that's been in the ground for years. The plants grow stronger and sturdier over time, more able to withstand times of stress. Also, the plants in this example were located in a northern area of the United States (Cape Cod), where hydrangeas can tolerate more sun than they could in a more southern location.

Moisture

The moisture needs of lacecaps are important considerations. Ideally, the soil should be organically rich, evenly moist, and well draining. Soaker hoses are much better than overhead watering, by getting the needed water directly to the roots. Overhead watering can lead to fungal infections on the foliage. A layer of mulch will help keep the soil evenly moist. If you are adding a lacecap to your garden, you can test drainage by filling the hole you dig for the plant with water and observing how quickly it disappears into the ground. In a sandy soil, the water will be gone in a flash (add organic matter before planting). In a heavy clay soil, the water will sit there for a long time. A plant put there would be a prime candidate for root rot and the eventual (sooner rather than later) demise of the plant. Clay soil needs to be amended with organic matter. Then do the drainage test again.

Watering advice is the same for lacecaps and mopheads, both indoors and outdoors. Rich soil is kept evenly moist; not too wet and not too dry.

❮ Good drainage is essential for hydrangeas. This ingenious arrangement of pot within pot within pot helps prevent two common watering problems: overwatering and underwatering. The plant in the small pot is placed inside the larger plastic pot, sized so that the bottom of the smaller pot is suspended a few inches above the bottom of the larger pot, allowing good drainage of excess water. A wicking arrangement can draw moisture from the bottom of the larger pot, if needed. The combined pots are then set into the decorative pot.

The larger plastic pot, shown here with the smaller pot tucked inside, has a hole in the side that allows excess water to drain away. The hole is located high enough that a reservoir of water remains in the bottom of the pot.

Soaker hoses are an excellent watering method for hydrangeas. Water is directed to the roots and can be timed to keep the soil evenly moist. A layer of mulch over this arrangement serves to cover the hoses and help retain the moisture.

Mother Nature can be fickle in her watering schedule. Rain does not always arrive when needed. Soaker hoses are a good way to provide supplementary moisture when needed.

Fertilizer

In early spring, apply an organic, time-release fertilizer such as Osmocote or Holly Tone. Other forms of fertilizer require more-frequent applications, some as often as every two weeks, whereas the time-release forms can provide nutrients for up to three months. No matter what kind of fertilizer you choose to use, make sure you water it well, to help it get down to the roots.

Don't make the mistake of overfertilizing, thinking you're giving the plant an extra boost. Instead, it could be detrimental to the plant. Follow package directions for best results.

Soil Amendments

There are three components to the subject of soil amendments. We will address each in turn.

Soil Amendments before Planting

The ideal soil for hydrangeas is rich with organic material, is moist but not overly wet, and drains well. When you start digging the hole and you discover that the soil is less than ideal (both sandy soil and heavy clay soil are less than ideal), try to mix in such amendments as compost, shredded leaves, and well-rotted manure. A garden center will direct you to the kind of materials that will help at planting time.

Soil Amendments after Planting

You can improve the quality of the soil surrounding an existing planting without having to dig up the plant. In the fall, top-dress with 2 inches of compost or mulch. These will gradually improve the soil below. This can be done annually.

Soil Amendments for Color Changes

If you want to change the color of your hydrangea flowers from blue to pink or from pink to blue, you need to add products to the soil: aluminum sulfate (for blues) or lime (for pinks). Do not expect instant results. It is easier to control color changes in a container than in the garden.

Please note that white hydrangeas will not change color with soil amendments. Nature might affect the color when the flowers age, but you will not be able to make a white hydrangea either blue or pink.

When using either aluminum sulfate or lime, make sure you follow the package directions. Too much can be toxic to the plant.

Winter Protection

You may have heard the term "winter protection" applied to the care of hydrangeas, and indeed, many strategies are employed to try to help those flower buds survive long enough to produce flowers. Plants are wrapped with chicken wire or some other structure, and these cages are filled with straw or leaves and wrapped with materials such as burlap or frost cloth. Many rules have to be followed. The plants shouldn't be covered until they go dormant (wait for all the leaves to fall off). Protection has to be sturdy enough to withstand howling wind. The plants must be uncovered when the new spring growth appears, *but* one must be alert to possible frost advisories, at which point protection must be reapplied. Many gardeners choose to simply hope for the best. Others turn to the container solution. Lacecaps grown in containers can be brought into a sheltered place for the winter, thus protecting the tender flower buds.

If you have had a problem with a lack of blooms due to weather complications, you might want to plant remontant varieties. "Remontant" means flowering more than once in a single season. These remontant (also called reblooming) varieties bloom both on old and new wood. If the flower buds formed on old wood fail to survive the winter, or they get zapped by a spring thaw/freeze cycle, rebloomers will form buds on new growth.

Most of the remontant hydrangeas are mopheads. Twist-n-Shout®, in the Endless Summer® collection, was the first remontant lacecap. Other remontant lacecaps include Pop Star™, Tuff Stuff™, Tuff Stuff Ah-Ha®, Tuff Stuff Top Fun™, and Let's Dance Can Do!®.

The general rule for plant success is to put the right plant in the right place. Follow the recommendations above and be rewarded with a beautiful, low-maintenance lacecap hydrangea that will give you years of garden pleasure.

You can tell by the shutters on the side of this house that it is a neglected property. In contrast, this lacecap shrub is thriving. The size of the plant indicates it is a well-established plant, and its health suggests it was placed in ideal conditions. Getting those conditions right goes a long way toward letting the plant succeed on its own with only minimal care.

Lacecaps overlooking Nantucket Harbor

CHAPTER 10

Lacecap
BEAUTY

Lacecap hydrangeas add beauty galore to the home garden. The photos selected for this chapter show lacecaps in many different stages of development, demonstrating that you can't go wrong with lacecaps; they will provide months of viewing pleasure. Let your eyes linger on these images. After doing do, you'll likely not question whether you should add a lacecap or two (or many!) to your garden, but how soon you can do so.

This lacecap shrub was planted right next to a driveway where it could be viewed easily.

Lacecaps can be spotted all over the island of Martha's Vineyard.

Lush lacecaps on the island of Nantucket

Lacecaps come in many colors. All are beautiful.

Blue lacecaps looking classic in a white metal container

'Strawberries and Cream'

'Tokyo Delight'

The sepals on some lacecaps are highly serrated, giving them a frilly appearance.

Double flowers on an early-spring bloom

'Blue Deckle'

Some varieties produce colors that are muted and restful.

The vibrant color on this one calls out for attention.

A classic blue lacecap

Get as close as possible to lacecap blooms to truly appreciate their beauty.

This late-season lacecap continues to look beautiful even with the fertile flowers exploding open in the center of the bloom.

Let's Dance® Starlight

A tricolor effect. Purple sepals with blue tinges surrounding the white eyes of the florets.

A two-toned effect with two shades of blue

Large sepals on the large flower heads of 'Fasan'

Sterile sepals floating gracefully around the perimeter of the bloom

Double flowers in soft lavender

A fresh bloom in June

An early-spring bloom with a soft creamy color intermixed with clear blue

'Lanarth White'

A graceful side view

'Beauté Vendômoise'

Blue with white accents, viewed from above

'Bluebird'

A lush lacecap shrub viewed from a restaurant terrace on Cape Cod

Lacecap close-ups reveal many beautiful details.

'Juno'

Let's Dance Diva!®

Index

Tuff Stuff™

Author Bio

Joan Harrison has been passionate about hydrangeas for over 30 years, prompting her to tour gardens featuring hydrangeas in England, Wales, France, Belgium, Ireland, and the Azores. A master gardener, writer, photographer, and speaker, she has been featured at the 2015 International Hydrangea Conference at Heritage Gardens, the Boston Flower Show, the Newport Flower Show, and Hydrangea University, the kickoff event for the annual Cape Cod Hydrangea Festival. She is the author of *Heavenly Hydrangeas: A Practical Guide for the Home Gardener*; *Hydrangeas: Cape Cod and the Islands*; and *Marvelous Mopheads: Hydrangeas for Home & Garden*. As the founding president of the Cape Cod Hydrangea Society, she proposed and implemented the goal of creating a hydrangea display garden on Cape Cod, now a featured attraction during the Cape's annual Hydrangea Festival. She lives in Plymouth, Massachusetts.